Winninger's 49 concepts for thinking smart will do so much more than help your business get focused, it will help you get personal clarity! — Ken Blanchard, Co-author *The One Minute Manager and Customer Mania*

Thom Winninger captures the essence of thinking smart, making the right decision at the right time, and "hitting The Bullseye." — Kendrick B. Melrose, Chairman & CEO, The Toro Co.

Winninger's purpose is clear; showing how to define what you do so clearly that you can command and retain Market Dominance! — Gary Johnson, Vice President, Patterson Co.

Winninger's concept are clear; showing how to define what you do so clearly that you can obtain and sustain a competitive advantage in your business. — Filemon Logez, Regional Senior Vice President, Comcast

Thom has done it again! His brilliant creative and practical mind gives us a book with numerous, easily implementable ideas to differentiate ourselves from our competitors and get and keep our customers for life. You'll profit many times over from Thom's powerful insight! — Dr. Tony Alessandra, Author of *Collaborative Selling* and *The Platinum Rule*

Thom his latest work. Thom delivers powerful insight that anyone can benefit from in the quest to be best. Bullseye will help you take your thinking to the next level. — Mark Sanborn, Author of *The Fear Factor: How Passion in Your Work & Life Can Make the Ordinary Extraordinary*

I found the concept to be insightful and on the mark. As the Director of learning and executive development, you are providing me the tools to help our executives grow our business. In short, Bullseye presents 49 brilliant concepts to help our organization makes the right critical choices in providing the greatest value to our customers. — Chris Carr, Boston Coach Corp

Read it, believe it, live it! He captures the essence of thinking smart, and making the best choices. — Keith Sherman, President, Dalton Advertising, Inc.

Winninger's Bullseye transends traditional leadership strategies and commands market dominance. — Aaron M. Schoeneberger, Director of Marketing Superior Walls of America

Winninger's purpose has become my passion: Define what you do so clearly that you defy your competition and command center stage in your market. — Dianna Booher, Author of *From Contact to Contact* and *Communicate with Confidence*

What a gift! Finally a book that helps you get out of the market clutter to find a bullseye worth hitting. The Smart Question and proven truths will give you a focus that will take you to market leadership. Devour this book now! — Terry Paulson, PhD, Author of *The Dinner! The Political Conversation Your Mother told you Never to Have*

Bullseye is critical to help organizations realize that just hitting the target is not good enough, you must hit the Bullseye! — Stacy Tetshner, CAE, Executive Vice President/ CEO National Speakers Assoc.

BULLSEYE!

BOOK 1
THINK SMART

THOMAS J. WINNINGER

ST. THOMAS PRESS
EDINA, MN

Published by St. Thomas Press
5637 Interlachen Circle
Edina, MN 55436

Publisher's Cataloging-in-Publication Data
Winninger, Thomas J.

Bullseye!. Book 1, Think smart / Thomas J. Winninger. – Edina, MN : St. Thomas Press, 2006.

p. ; cm.
ISBN: 0-9638735-3-9
ISBN13: 978-0-9638735-3-8

1. Marketing-Management. 2. Marketing-Planning. 3. Marketing. I. Title.
HF5415.13 .W56 2005
658.8-dc22   2005933915

Book production and coordination by Jenkins Group, Inc.
www.bookpublishing.com

Interior design by Chad Miller
Cover design by George Foster

Printed in the United States of America
10   09 08 07 06 • 5 4 3 2 1

CONTENTS

Achieving Focus

PREFACE

Market leaders are all different. The Starbucks, the eBays, the Godivas, and the Barnes & Nobles do things differently. At Starbucks, it's not the coffee, but what they do to the coffee, how they treat the coffee, the environment in which they serve the coffee, that sets the company apart. They have pulled it all together. They have hit the bullseye, and they continue to hit it again and again.

But this book is not as much about how companies capture and sustain market leadership as it is about you, how you can not only define your bullseye, but hit it, again and again. That is, how you can attain and sustain market leadership, so that you and your company will be the one whom everyone thinks of as the first source, the category authority who is the market leader.

One reason companies fail to capture market leadership is that they live in a world of false perceptions. They think that simply doing something faster or better will catapult them ahead of their competitors and help them reap market rewards. They pursue speed or quality for the sake of speed and quality.

The world today is cluttered with quality products and better ideas. It is cluttered with companies that have lots of targets related to getting the job done faster and better. But those companies have no bullseye. They are working without a final destination in mind. They think that if they just continue to do something faster and better they will get somewhere. Owners, managers, and CEOs think they can achieve success if they just keep working harder, selling more, and creating more. As more and more start-up companies enter the market each year, those owners, managers, and CEOs find themselves running faster and farther but making very little progress. They are actually losing ground in their markets.

> **Truth:** Improving the quality of an action doesn't in and of itself ensure success.

In other words, just getting better at doing something doesn't mean you are making progress. Simply serving better bread or offering better merchandise or manufacturing a better automobile brake is like shooting arrows with your eyes closed.

It only results in a tired arm and an empty quiver. I'm reminded of a manufacturer of eight-track tapes. Making better eight-track tapes didn't save the company when a competitor began to produce cassette tapes, and then CDs, then DVDs, now streaming internet video. Another example that reflects this truth well was provided by the ancient Greeks. The Greeks ceased to exist as a dominant world authority because they spent their time trying to perfect the process of thinking for the sake of thinking, rather than targeting their thinking at specific issues, not unlike great organizations today who think, or strategically plan, without implementing any of their thinking.

The world is full of business failures. Based on current trends, during the next eight years, 72 percent of businesses operating today in the US will fail in their attempt to succeed. The major threat they face is lack of differentiation. Products and services begin to look alike, slipping into commoditization. Almost every sector, from legal services and LASIK surgery to bagel shops and educational institutions, is facing this challenge.

This tragic market situation is caused by an ignorant competitive instinct that I refer to as the Processionary Caterpillar Syndrome. Six caterpillars are born on a leaf. They don't develop sight for some time, but they need to eat. Each caterpillar crawls around on the leaf, blindly searching for food and feeling its way, until it discovers another caterpillar. Instinct tells it that the other caterpillar knows where the food is because it's moving, so the first caterpillar attaches itself to the second. What it doesn't know is that the caterpillar it now is attached to can't see either.

So it continues, until each of the six caterpillars is attached to the rear end of another. And each thinks the one ahead of it is the leader and knows where it's going. Eventually, however, the lead caterpillar finds the rear end of the caterpillar that is last in line and attaches itself to that caterpillar's rear end. Now the six caterpillars have formed a circle, each following the one ahead and thinking it is getting somewhere. In reality, none of them are leaders, they are merely following their own rear ends.

We see similar situations with people and companies, one copying another, thinking the other knows something they don't know. The minute one person or company does something different, another copies it, followed by another and another, much like the processionary caterpillar. They don't realize that a real leader will always have more success with a new concept because he is attached to the real customer, while the followers are merely attached to each other. Their vision is blurred; they are not thinking smart. I'm not suggesting that the followers can't have some success, but it usually comes because they enhance or change something about the way the leader is already doing things. If you play out the scenario, by the time the last follower has copied what the leader has done, the leader is off in a new and different direction based on his understanding of the changing needs of his real customers.

To capture and sustain market leadership today, to hit the bullseye, you must master the three rings of the target. Ring one: Think Smart. Ring two: Create Value. Ring three: Build Cultures of Difference. Because mastering these rings is so critical, I have chosen to address each in an individual book. The *BULLSEYE!* trilogy focuses on aiming at, and hitting, the bullseye, and doing so on a consistent basis. It is about bringing clarity to what you are doing and where you want to go. It is about thinking smarter. It is about creating distinctive value that captures and sustains market attention. It is about building a culture of difference, about being, not just doing that define your whole organization.

Utilizing my twenty-five years of experience of working inside some fifteen hundred market leaders, I will demonstrate to you in the *BULLSEYE!* trilogy how to apply strategic market operatives that will ensure you can shift effectively in the most challenging and quickly changing markets. I will

BULLSEYE!

show you how to create true differentiation, while
becoming more innovative in the ways you target
your real, and changing, customer. That customer is
the mover and shaker, dictating who wins and who
loses. That customer is part of the shifting paradigm
that continually challenges the position of any
market leader.

Through the *BULLSEYE!* trilogy, you will learn
how to insulate yourself and your organization
from the mistakes made by the processionary
caterpillars. You will learn how to find and define
the bullseye. You will discover how to use fewer
arrows and less effort to hit the bullseye and you
will learn how to do it consistently. In this new
world, where the rules of graduate business schools
are being broken everyday, shooting arrows in the
conventional way, in hopes of hitting the target, is
ineffective. There is just too many organizations
who are changing the rules!

The actions you take as a result of what you
learn from the *BULLSEYE!* trilogy will move you
closer to an overwhelming return on your activity.
The three books in this series celebrate the fact that,
if you understand the three-ring process of think
smart, create distinctive value, and build a culture
of difference, you have a good chance of changing
the rules in your favor!

Introduction

In the next twenty years, we will benefit from more economic opportunities than we did in the last fifteen hundred years, ever since the Fall of the Roman Empire. Never before in recorded history has man been able to develop so many individual products and services and, as a result of his creativity, build a place where people can live so well. At the same time, the instinctive creativity of man has created a marketplace that is confused with products, services, and technologies. Instant communication and seamless transportation systems have brought the peoples and businesses of the world closer together. Yet in this age of unparalleled opportunity, man continues on a downward spiral in his ability to think successfully, to think wisely, to think smartly.

Truth: Thinking smart is the only true differentiator.

In a time when almost everything can be copied or imitated, two things cannot be copied: the quality of the mind and the process of thinking. Thinking smart, making better decisions and applying those decisions to create a culture of difference, is the only true differentiator, yet we spend the least amount of time on it. When we do spend time thinking, we fail to attach it to purpose, to definition, to outcome, to clarity.

Today's global environment and technology provides us with access to more information than ever before, but customers continue to cry out, not pleading for more products and services, but for the kind that address the uniqueness of their individualized needs. "Give us products and services with purpose," they demand. Most businesses are missing this critical point. They made the mistake of believing that technology and globalization would make it easier for them to satisfy the needs of the customer and, in so doing, maintain growth and profitability. In the last four years of the Twentieth Century, they came to realize that technology, specifically the Internet, in and of itself would not support market leadership. While global companies have used the opening of new markets to fund losses in their old markets, they have failed to continue to innovate, to create new opportunities along with those new markets.

The vast majority of organizations simply have not learned how to think smart. They do not know the difference between being and doing, between thinking and acting.

Market leaders didn't capture their positions by asking, "How can we do it better than the others?" They captured their positions, they hit the bullseye, by asking, "How can we do it differently?"

> **Truth:** Doing things differently gets more attention than doing things better.

American car companies didn't save themselves by building better cars. Yes, that might have contributed, but lease programs, extended warranties, and rebates are what really got the customers' attention and changed the way customers made decisions about their car purchases. The continued focus on "better" as a buying motive has confused today's customers about what to buy, how to buy it, what to pay for it, and who to buy it from. That is exacerbated by every organization that claims to do it better or at a lower cost. Customers are confused about what "better" means. They have given up trying to figure it out. They are attracted to things that appear to be different, things that challenge them to figure it out, and things that bring a different view to their world.

As you begin this study, I challenge you to accept an important revelation that I have been inspired by for more than fifteen years. It is this: Successful organizations don't need more ideas; they need to understand the *truths* at the foundation of market leadership. They need clarity, the ability to see clearly the true purpose of their product and its opportunity to have value in the mind and heart of a specific targeted customer.

BULLSEYE! is a clearly defined, sustainable market differentiator. Hitting the bullseye results from an ability to draw your entire resources into a single focus that creates clarity about who you are, what you are doing, who your are doing it for, what makes you different and why it is important.

I weary of books that simply share idea upon idea. People eventually come to the realization that they don't need any more ideas; they need ideas that work, ideas that sustain success. Ideas that work over that long term are ideas that are based on truths, the foundational concepts from which the ideas emerge. Truths create the foundation for beliefs. Whether you call them truths or business principles, it's impossible to argue with them. Those who ignore these truths and believe that going back to the basics is the best strategy will only get to where they already have been, and they will get there faster.

The concepts in the *BULLSEYE!* trilogy are based on truths, not just ideas. It is imperative that you base your thinking and your actions on truths. Many of the truths that I base my work on have been around for almost two thousand years. These truths come from some of the greatest minds in history: Aristotle, St. Augustine, Thomas Aquinas, and Leonardo da Vinci. They are market-relevant truths. An example of one most often applied by market leaders is the "is" versus "does" truth.

> **Truth:** It's not what you sell, it's what the customer buys, that drives market leadership. In other words, it's not what it is, but what it does.

Do customers buy a cup of coffee at Starbucks, or do they buy an escape to an environment where they can enhance their feelings of liberation around like-minded people while connecting to a world of Internet information with a wireless service? You be the judge. Is Godiva a chocolate or is it a gift? Hallmark has built its market leadership on the fact that it isn't the card itself that is important, but the act on the part of the purchaser that says he or she "cared enough to send the very best."

This truth can be applied to any product or service. For example, are you performing LASIK surgery, or are you improving vision and liberating people from the cumbersome burden of glasses and contacts? Ophthalmologists can argue with my reasoning, but they can't argue with the market.

They have turned vision improvement into a commodity procedure called LASIK surgery, and they advertise the price to drive market share. There is a reason that Harley-Davidson has maintained market dominance, why Starbucks easily could have ten thousand stores within the next few years, why FOX News has become the most dominant player in the up to the minute fair-minded news reporting sector.

As part of the introduction to this series, I point out five underlying market trends that are causing confusion for organizations seeking market leadership. The first is globalization. It's an opportunity and a curse at the same time. The upside is that globalization affords us the ability to capture markets we were unable to serve in the past, new markets that are not saturated with competitive products, and to appeal to a fresh audience with a not-too-fresh product. On the downside, globalization can strip a organization's profitability and give it false hope that the new land will afford them insights for restructuring the old land. In reality, it merely blinds that company to the truism that the product it has needs to be reinvented, not just taken to a new market.

The second trend is polarization. On one end of every market there are organizations that use "low price" as a differentiator, while on the other end there are those organizations that use "value" as a differentiator. No organizations will be in the middle. Polarization refers to the fact that there are no organizations that can maintain a "middle-of-the-market" position. The "middle-of-the-market" organizations get caught in trying to sell high value at a low price, a strategy that provides no margin to cover the cost of doing business. This type of strategy is simply unfeasible. The main contributor to the demise of the middle-of-the-market company that tried to give "old-fashioned" service at a low price, thinking volume was the Internet. Customers are exposed to more information about any single product or service than ever before. Real-time quotes, Web shopping, and online auctions have given them the ability to gather price comparison information with the click of a mouse. I do not agree with those who say the Internet will be the buying portal for most products and services in the future, just as I disagreed with those who twenty years ago declared that Wal-Mart would become everyone's retailer or that television would replace movies.

I do agree, however, that the Internet will be an information portal for most products and services. Research shows that the majority of purchasing customers turns to the Internet for information about products and services and then consider alternate stores to make their purchases. Today's markets are convergent: the Internet is driving store sales, and stores are driving Internet activity. This is why Dell opened retail computer stores.

The third trend creating market confusion is proliferation, the ever-increasing number of new products and services entering the market every year. A store with 120,000 SKUs, or individual products on the shelf, is not uncommon today in many trade sectors. How many different sizes or colors or flavors of ketchup can we offer the buying public? Proliferation confuses the customer. It's like Ralph sitting on a couch after dinner, armed with a remote and continuously clicking through channel after channel in an attempt to find a program that will hold his interest for more than fifteen seconds.

Proliferation leads to the fourth trend: commoditization. Any product or service, from chocolate and LASIK surgery to technology and legal services, can end up being a commodity. A commodity is a product that has no singular value because so many other products like it are in the market and are easily accessible. Market leaders must think smart so that they can insulate themselves against this trend.

The fifth trend is a globally maturing population. In most developed markets this maturing or aging population has more discretionary money to spend than ever before and could affect the market popularity of almost any product and service. This age bubble will becoming dominant. That means that, no matter what you're producing, the profile of this group is affecting the market appeal of your product and, thereby, its perceived value.

In this first of the *BULLSEYE!* trilogy books, the focus is on think smart, differently, not just how to think smart as a process, but how to think smart as an outcome. The difference between process and outcome is the difference between tactical and strategic. It is like fixing an existing thing versus creating a new thing. It is the difference between graduate schools that are giving out degrees and graduate schools that are reinventing the way students think. Thinking smart for outcome is the ability to create, to innovate, to clarify your differentiator. Your differentiator is that *one thing* that captures and sustains market leadership. Identifying your *one thing* will be covered in great depth in this series.

In addition to remembering the five trends, there are also five basic principles about thinking smart that you should keep in mind as you work your way through this first book in the *BULLSEYE!* trilogy series:

1. There is a truth behind every successful idea! For example, theology is a truth. Thomas Aquinas, a student of Aristotle, espoused it. Basically, it stated that the better defined your

goal, the easier it is to identify the actions it will take to achieve that goal. Put simply, if you know your destination, the road to get there becomes obvious.

2. Thinking smart and being knowledgeable is not the same thing. It's the difference between someone who knows everything and someone who can make the right decisions at the right time, and hit the bullseye.

3. Mental and physical clutter reduces the potential of thinking smart. Most people cannot think smart in an environment of clutter, whether you have too much on your mind, too much on your agenda, or too much on your desk.

4. Smart questions, not smart assumptions, lead to thinking smart. Most thinking fails because the thinker has already defined the assumption. Rather than questioning the assumption, he or she is trying to prove it. For example, the assumption that if you make a higher quality product, you will capture market leadership has, over time, proven erroneous, but many organizations still base their future on it. The truth is that being different, not being better, has led more often to market leadership. Throw out the assumption!

5. Converging patterns lead to thinking smart. There is a principle that Leonardo da Vinci called *Connessione*. It means recognition of interconnectedness in things and ideas. Today it is referred to as the "it's a small world" theory, mistakenly suggesting that such things are only a coincidence. But things that work are usually connected to other things that work, and things that don't work are often not connected to anything. One of the reasons that Edison was so successful was that he had so many similar experiments going at once the connectivity helped him reach the obvious conclusions. Thinking smart is often nothing more than acknowledging connections.

Success is supported by almost invisible seamless system that sustains long-term market leadership. Organizations that consistently hit the bullseye include 3M, John Deere, Kohler, and Harley-Davidson.

This first book of the *BULLSEYE!* trilogy includes forty-nine concepts for thinking smart. These concepts are not sequenced in a process order, but rather in a way that will stimulate your thinking. *Think Smart* is the first in the series, because doing so is the only true differentiator.

Market Smart? Take the BULLSEYE Quiz...

1. Thinking Smart requires you to:
   A. Make smart assumptions.
   B. Know smart people.
   C. Ask smart questions.
   D. All of the above.

2. What causes confusion?
   A. Too many goals and objectives.
   B. Not understanding your customers.
   C. Globalization.
   D. All of the above.

Answers: winninger.com/bullseyequiz

BEING SMART

1   It's Not the Target, It's the *BULLSEYE!*

Thinking smart is a process that helps you zero in on actions that achieve a desired outcome. Thinking smart presupposes that as part of the process you have defined the right outcome, the overriding objective, the right desired end. Thinking smart can be equated with making the right decisions, doing the right things, taking the right steps. For the sake of this study, the desired end, or overriding objective, is market leadership. If the overriding objective is to be the market leader, you must decide what that means and how you will measure your arrival, hitting the bullseye. Looking at a personal example: if your overriding objective is to have a great family vacation, how will you measure that? Is it how the kids behaved? Is it the unique experiences you encountered or how cheaply you got by? Thinking smart means you have the ability to set your sights on some *one thing*, even though it might seem out of the ordinary or unconventional, that brings you to a point of determination or success. Thinking smart isn't having all the right answers at all the right times. It is having the courage and discipline to stay focused and to use all the resources available to you to hit your mark, the bullseye.

Although it's not an event I normally would tune in to, I watched the archery competition during the Summer Olympics. It's not a competition that involves speed, raw human strength, handsprings, or fleetness of foot. It isn't flashy or accompanied by flag-waving, chanting, or enthusiastic fans. But it does, I discovered as I watched, require extreme concentration, single-mindedness, and focus. The competitors were fixated on the small dot in the center of a relatively large target. Nothing distracted them. They looked at nothing but the bullseye, the center of the target. They focused intently on that little spot until, with a barely perceptible movement, they released the arrow, pleased to see it pierce the center. I gained new appreciation for the extreme discipline their focus required. I liken it to the ability of a company, in the midst of all they could do, to select the *one thing* they should do that will, more that any other thing, catapult them to the center stage of their marketplace.

Target Practice: Thinking of all the things you could provide for your customer, what is the *one thing*, the one reason, they would do business with you?

② Why Be Intelligent When You Can Be Smart?

Research proves that intelligence doesn't necessarily equal smart thinking. Intelligence is like the engine of an automobile. As Edward de Bono says in his book, *Thinking Course*, horsepower doesn't necessarily equal performance. More than anything else, the ability to think, and to think effectively, results in the skills necessary to drive the car of intelligence.

It's also important to note that thinking, in and of itself, doesn't necessarily generate good thinking over time. It's like garbage in, garbage out. If my process for thinking and analyzing and identifying and aiming at the bullseye is flawed from the beginning, or becomes flawed, no matter how many arrows I shoot at what I think is the target, the likelihood that I ever will hit a bullseye is almost nonexistent. If I haven't developed the correct process for thinking smart, then I, like most companies, think the best way out of my dilemma is just to shoot as many arrows as I can and hope I hit something: a new and successful product, a process, or a marketing strategy.

Studies show that the brain, or mind, is like a muscle. The more I use it, the stronger it becomes. But I want to strengthen it in the right way. People who train themselves to see things other people don't see develop a natural reflex that allows them to continue to do so. Two people will look at the same picture and see something different in it. One person will see the broad view, while the other sees the narrow view. Interestingly enough, over time, the person who sees the narrow view might very well be the person who hits the bullseye.

> ***Target Practice:*** Of all the things you know about your customer, your product, and your market, what is the *one thing* that is most important (for example your customer wants safety, your product is durables, your market is price competitive) in each category to your becoming the market leader?

3 Is It the Forest or the Trees?

Being smart and thinking smart comes down to working with perceptions, some true, some false. Market leaders look for the forest to find a tree, rather than looking for a tree to find the forest. They don't come up with a product and then try to prove whether or not the market will support it. They attach themselves to a great market to discover its needs.

Wendy's created an advertising program and spent more than $30 million trying to answer the question, "Where's the beef?" What's interesting is that research would show that, at the time, no one was interested in the beef. Beef consumption was declining nationally. But the folks at Wendy's were out to prove the perception that people wanted a better burger, and that a better burger meant more beef. Meanwhile, while Wendy's was looking for the beef, McDonald's was looking for the customer and trying to identify the number-one unsatisfied need of that customer.

False, or assumed, perceptions can be deadly to smart thinking. Early mathematicians believed the earth was flat; others believed it was the center of the universe. Both perceptions limited discovery. People who thought the earth was flat were afraid that, if they went out exploring, they eventually would fall off it. How often do you or your company make false perceptions, and then operate under those perceptions?

> **Truth:** The purification of a false perception does not increase market value.

If you believe that simply making your product better will result in an increase in market leadership and market share, and will position you for higher margins and increased profits, you're wrong. It's rather like the eccentric inventor who spends countless hours laboring over the minute details of his prized creation. He tests and tests, tools and retools, only to find that when put to the test in real life, the invention fails to capture the interest of the consumer. Having a better product will not necessarily result in success in the market. Don't run yourself into the ground seeking new ways to do things better than the other guy just for the sake of quality. If you are determined to focus on increasing quality, at least do it to an object that in some way is serving a changing need of the marketplace.

> **Target Practice:** What *one thing* makes your product stand out in the market, the *one thing* that, if several competitive products were lined up in a row, would make yours draw immediate attention? (Next, replace the word product with service and answer the question again.)

4 Thinking for the Sake of Thinking Gets You Nowhere

If we ask why the Greeks lost their position as a world power, we would probably discover this: they believed that the process of thinking, simply for the sake of thinking, was of value. The Greeks' downfall was that, other than the purification of the thinking process, they had no objective.

The company that seeks a quality product for the sake of quality, rather than quality for the sake of the customer's satisfaction or for the sake of pure market leadership, will not be successful.

> ***Target Practice:*** Practice a group-think. Bring no less than five and no more than eight people together from different departments or backgrounds to a small group discussion. Draw straws to determine who will be the leader. Identify the seven or eight things that make your product (or service) the most attractive in the market; next, prioritize them in order of importance to the customer. If you cannot come to an agreement on the priority, ask the customer. You should have done that in the first place.

5 Smart Thinking Is a Process of Discovery

More than anything else, the ability to think smart is the ability to discover, research, clarify, and then apply. It truly comes down to broadening creative questioning, gathering information, and then sifting through the information to discover what's left in the sieve. Your ability to discover is a system that is based on your ability to not only listen, but also to ask key questions, and to gather information other people are not gathering. For example, how many times do companies research the requests they get from customers for things the company does not do?

> **Truth:** The future of your company is hiding in the requests from your best customers for things that you do not do.

Companies that listen to the changing needs of their premium customers are companies that discover powerful perceptions. They are capable of being more creative than their competitors, because they understand that those requests are driving market intelligence, and they open their minds to them. A good example is a hotel guest who asks, "Why do I need to check in if I don't need to check out?" Leading hotel chains have used sophisticated technology during the past few years to make it possible for most customers, or guests, to just say "goodbye." If the bill is correct, guests can simply pick up the phone, press 8, approve the bill, and be on their way.

Research shows that the greatest frustration premium customers have is with the check-in process. The hotel chain that wants to be a leader with businesspeople and repeat customers would do well to develop a process that, simply stated, would allow them to tell guests, "Go to your room; don't stop at the front desk." Marriott has a simple process that it offers its Marquis customers. When those customers arrive at the hotel, their accounts have been set up, their rooms are ready, and they can skip the typical check-in process altogether.

Let's think outside the box, or out of the hotel room, so to speak. When a customer books a room by phone or on the Internet, he could be checked in by the reservations clerk, who takes his credit card number, accesses the credit card information, confirms the room number and the particulars about that room, gives the customer the room number and provides a code that will be keyed into that room's lock after noon on the day that guest will arrive. This would be music to any guest's ears. This is creative thinking, creative processing, being different, thinking smart—hitting the bullseye.

Target Practice: Over a period of time, track the requests you get from your customers for things that you don't offer. Be sensitive to the type of customer asking for a specific thing and the frequency of the request. If it becomes obvious that there is *one thing* your best customer asks for on a frequent basis that you don't provide, the objective would be to list the actions necessary to begin offering it successfully. How? Where? When? How much? How many?

Market Smart? Take the BULLSEYE Quiz...

3. Your perceptions:
   A. Are usually true.
   B. Limit your outcomes
   C. Often get in the way of smart thinking.
   D. All of the above.

Answers: winninger.com/bullseyequiz

USING INTUITION

 Inspiration Can Help or Hinder

All of us have, at some time, had an inspired thought that seems to just come out of the blue. Intuition is the mind taking experiences and translating them into ideas. That inkling of intuition comes from some experience that speaks to us. It might say there is a better or different way to do something or it might say that there is something missing. Intuition can be more of a hindrance than a help. It can trap you into believing that it should dictate the way to live your life or to capture market share. People sometimes get an idea and they are off and running in almost any direction. Intuition can create problems if it results from experiences that haven't been successful, in which case the intuitive ideas it generates don't turn out to be successful either. If we don't use intuition correctly to inspire our creativity, we will fall short of success. On the other hand, if we disregard intuition altogether, we will all end up being, as Einstein said, a society that honors the rational mind rather than the creative mind. Intuition can be effective only if there is a process of tracking it back to an experience and validating not only the value of the intuition, but also the market value of the idea.

Intuition Can Be Confirmed

If most of us had to wait for intuition to inspire us to some process or opportunity, it would change the way we do business; it would be years before great ideas were turned into action that would allow us to capture market leadership. Most businesses evolve out of an idea that came from another business or experience. These ideas are called derivatives—for example, making a better or different mousetrap.

Since intuition is an outgrowth of experiences, it is a fallacy to believe that people are born with a high degree of intuition. It would be truer to state that some people are more inherently inquisitive than other people and that inquisitiveness is the fuel that drives intuition. Considering the definition of intuition as experiences turned into ideas, a person without a great number of experiences typically will not be very intuitive. And a person who does not develop intuitive instinct as a skill will be not be as innovative. If we make the assumption that all people are in one way or another intuitive—that is, spontaneous thoughts come to them about things they are experiencing—then achieving true focus would be to move to a higher level or quality of intuition. This can be done by enhancing experiences. Getting out of the business box, so to speak, by visiting businesses that are outside of your industry but who have some of the same kind of customers.

Those who have climbed Kilimanjaro see things other people don't see. Intuitions that you can bank on, that is, those which really have some substance, are subject to qualification, a process of analyzing the substance of the experiences that led to them. Intuition is not a process of collecting as much data on a subject as possible and then identifying priorities. It is not merely hoping that if you shoot enough arrows you will hit the bullseye. Intuition is like an instinct for noticing the unnoticed. What is obvious to one person is may be utterly obscure to another.

Jim Lind runs a BP Amoco service station in a relatively small Midwestern community. His focus on being observant in serving his customers brought him to a realization, an intuitive thought. *Why not offer full service to people with handicapped stickers in their windows?* Intuition, complemented by Jim's personal values and coupled with his experiences in the business, led him to this decision. At no additional charge, people with handicapped stickers would get full service at a regular self-service pump. Jim's experience had made him understand the value of offering individual attention to every customer at a self-service pump. This attention included, whenever possible, checking the oil, tire pressure, and windshield washer fluid while the customer pumped his own gas. The outcome of that was the realization that cars at the self-service pump often need often more attention. Even though they were pumping their own gas, customers appreciated the extra attention, and Jim enjoyed an incremental increase in per-transaction profitability.

⑧ Intuition Comes from Converging Clues

Intuition really comes from a set or pattern of clues that converge. In other words, the clues somehow connect. They end up in the same part of your mind with a common element and lead you to make a discovery based upon their dynamic. It is very similar with a creative mind. The creative mind tends to see patterns in its thinking that brings it to the identification of a focal point—a bullseye. It would follow something like this: a situation generates a clue, the clue becomes part of a pattern, the pattern leads to an idea or a response, and the response drives the situation. It becomes a circle. You could call it intuition, or discovery.

It happened to UPS as a result of a situation that had become a pattern. UPS observed the number of calls it was getting from customers for package tracking. As a result of that converging pattern, UPS developed package-handling software that eventually became the shipping department for its customers. Intuition helped UPS create and utilize a solution that provided its customers with not only a way to track packages, but also a way to ship the package themselves, using bar coding and integrated technologies. UPS changed the rules of doing business by making the customer more self-dependent, and at the same time more deeply connected to UPS.

> **Truth:** Intuition is an instinct for, noticing the unnoticed.

> **Target Practice:** Can you identify any repeated patterns in your business experience? Perhaps

something customers ask for on a regular basis, or a problem or challenge that repeats itself on a regular basis? Using intuition to be more creative can lead to thinking smart.

⑨ Don't Jump Ship Too Quickly

The smartest people are people who understand what they are really good at, their core skills or core talents, and then marry those things to the real and changing needs of the customer. The most significant needs of the customer are the enhanced needs. You could also refer to these enhanced needs as wants. You might not really need these things, but you want them. You need golf clubs to play a round of golf, but you might want a golf cart so you don't have to walk the course. The golf cart is an enhanced need. You need to check out of the hotel at the end of your stay, but you want to avoid waiting in the long line at the front desk to do it, enhanced need.

When a company identifies these enhanced needs, it often jumps too quickly into providing them. This frequently happens with the application of technology. Companies think that the mere addition of a certain kind of technology in the customer experience will serve an enhanced need. They typically fail when they use such reasoning, because the customer didn't need or want the technology, they needed or wanted what the *technology does.* Unfortunately, the temptation is to provide the technology rather that the application of the technology. Unable to identify the enhanced needs that will provide growth and market leadership, some companies simply go on an acquisition binge. They purchase other companies that are successful but are unrelated to their core business and core customers.

Example: A company that makes toolboxes for mechanics gets into the food processing business. That doesn't make any sense, because the cultures and product lines of the two businesses are different. But let's say the company is in the manufacturing management business. If that's the case, then the cultures should be similar. If you are following my line of thinking, it says this: make sure you understand what the core customer needs and wants.

> ***Target Practice:*** Do a 360-degree analysis. Think about what you really do for both the customer you want to capture and the customer you want to keep. Try to discern the unsatisfied needs of those customers.

I recently worked with a company that was in the facilities management business. They were convinced that they could manage any facility, so on any given day or in any given year, they were managing a manufacturing plant on one side of their business and a convention and visitors complex on another side of their business. Totally different core talent was required. There was no convergence, no relationship, between the facilities. After a few years, their intuition indicated that with a growing need for manufacturing facility management, they should simply spin off the event facility management part of their business. As a result of this, the business grew exponentially. The found their core, the ability to manage manufacturing facilities. Because what manufacturer wants to put all their effort into managing a facility? What they really want is to be really good at manufacturing. They want to be a specialist in the production process that takes place within the bricks-and-mortar building.

The lesson is this: quit thinking about every other organization you could be in and become a scholar of your own organization, your own customer. Everyone else's boat looks bigger. Everyone else's car looks fancier. Everyone else's job looks better, Every business idea looks more lucrative than yours, and every product or service, when you fixate on it long enough, will look like it's worth more than yours. Remember: think convergence, integration, core product, core service-think patterns. Think what originally inspired you to choose your particular product or service. Then, to be truly intuitive, go beyond that and move as close as you can to the need for it, the application of it, and away from the specification of it.

> ***Target Practice:*** List all the things you do that aren't related to your core product or service. What do you do that you could stop doing without it having a measurable effect on the size of your market or the quality of the relationship you have with your customer?

10 Think Application, Not Specification

More often than not, research stifles creativity and thinking smart, especially when the research focuses on the specification of the product rather than its application. So much research is focused on the "so-you-like-the-color" category that you miss the real value to the customer. That value is in the application of the product. A food manufacturer was so focused on whether the customer liked their products that they never realized the real reason they were losing market share: their drivers were always late making deliveries. For a number of years, I have talked about Michael Dell and the fact that his incredibly successful namesake company did an excellent job of focusing on the application of the technology. It focused on how the computer solved a problem for the customer. From my perspective, Dell never really got into the computer business. It was in the computer application business, or what I would like to call "deliverable technology." What Michael Dell asked himself was, "How do I get technologies that support the needs of the customer's applications into their hands as swiftly as possible, and then how do I effectively support them in the use of that technology?" When you bought a computer from Dell, it was like having an insourced geek, i.e., technical support person. Dell prided itself on not just being able to support the technology for the workability of the computer, but also the application of that technology.

> **Truth:** It is application, not specification, that drives market leadership.

The more companies move toward application of their product, the more intuitive and the smart they tend to be. Think of it in terms of what it *does* rather than what it *is*. Get out of the features and into the benefits.

Target Practice: Take one of your core products or services and list all of its possible benefits to the customer.

11 Get Out of Your Planner

It is amazing how we human beings condition ourselves regarding our perception of what constitutes being smart. Recently I was having lunch with a friend of mine in Chicago named Andy. Andy was so proud of his pocket PC. He didn't seem to realize that is was nothing more than a technology that gave him the capability to carry huge amounts of manageable data, or should I say unmanageable, but not necessarily relevant, data. He shared with me how he had started off with a binder-planner years ago. He had taken a class on how to write out everything that he needed to do and then prioritize it. He learned how break his list into down into blocks of similar activities and then prioritize each of the blocks of activities. In this way, he was sure that he was working on the number-one priority in the number-one category.

This allowed him to reduce his time and effort and gave him time to get more things done. He proudly shared with me how each day he rewrote or carried forward the things that he hadn't gotten done from the day before, ensuring that over a specific period of time, all of his priorities would be handled effectively. His story is echoed by an entire segment of society that has come to the same belief. They believe that getting a lot of things done has a linear relationship to thinking smart. It is my opinion that most really smart thinkers don't equate thinking smart with the amount of things that they get done. That doesn't mean that smart thinkers aren't productive, but the process is not linear. Market leaders don't consistently hit the mark by getting a lot done; they do it by getting the right thing done. They realize two important things: that managing priorities doesn't necessarily make you smart, and that the time it takes to manage activities that are not bullseye activities, or top-of-your-list activities, commands so many resources that you will never be smart.

Let me give you an example so that you can identify whether you are an activity type of person. The comment I often hear is, "I never get the things done that I think I need to get done." They hear a voice inside, a cry of intuition, saying, "Your routine is killing your ability to think smart."

Are you busy answering meaningless e-mails that get in your way of doing quality thinking? Either we are too busy doing things the way we've always done them, or we are too busy doing them the way some efficiency guru said we ought to do them. However, often the guru has never done what you do. If you have ten things that you think you need to do because someone once told you to make a list of ten things and then prioritize them, forget it. Listen to your intuition, that voice gnawing at you and telling you that one of those things is the thing. Make that thing the *one thing*. But that alone is not enough; you must eliminate the other things so that they are not crying out for attention. Realize that the reason you don't do that *one thing* is because there is so much more of the target you can shoot at. It is easier to just keep shooting arrows at the target randomly than to take the time to focus on the bullseye.

> **Truth:** It's the repetition of the tangible versus the importance of the intangible that draws my attention, Keeping me from success.

It happens to all of us sometimes: if there is a lot to do, we are easily drawn away from the most important things. Things that are tangible tend to draw your attention away from things that are important. A phone call is tangible, e-mail is tangible, paperwork is tangible. Thinking, on the other hand, is intangible, but thinking takes first place if you want to act smart. It is harder to block time for thinking.

> **Target Practice:** Practice selecting *one thing* from the list of all the things you need or want to do, and make that your main activity, not just a small part of all of your activities.

12 Don't Have the Answer before You Have the Question

Intuition will prove destructive if you let it be your guide. Intuition will lead you to believe the answer before you have the question. Imagine that you've identified a product gadget, or idea that you know is just the greatest thing in the whole universe. You've convinced yourself, with the help of your intuition, that it is worth a million dollars. You have the answer without the question. You have the cart before the horse. The John Deere plow company was in the same situation and was facing demise because of it. It had the greatest plow ever made. It was special and stainless steel and every farmer needed it. The company had a great answer, but no question—they had the cart before the horse. You see, the plow had to be pulled. The question was, "What can we pull the plow with so that everyone will buy our plows?" The answer, which Deere finally figured out, was the Waterloo Boy tractor. In this case, the answer to the question was not a horse, but a tractor. The John Deere company bought the Waterloo Boy tractor company and became the largest tractor, not plow, company in the world.

One of the biggest mistakes a company or individual can make is to put the thesis first and then seek to prove that thesis rather than collecting experiences and sifting through stimulus, putting the thesis at the end. My school experiences have shown me that most students will make a statement at the beginning of their paper and then spend the whole paper proving their point. Of course, there's nothing wrong with that if you are writing a paper for a professor or doing an analysis of something related to your business. But it's usually best to start with the question. I will give you an example based on a shopper. There is a certain type of price-conscious buyer who goes out and buys an item, knowing that he can return it, and then spends time shopping around for that same item at a lower price to prove or disprove the quality of his selection or his choice. Another person goes out and identifies choices, and in the process of identifying those choices comes up with a better choice, not just a lower price. I would prefer to spend my thinking time with the latter. The first person picks something, and then spends his time validating it. The second person keeps his options open while he is searching. I disagree with the speculation that Columbus sailed the ocean blue to prove that the world was round. He was sailing west, searching for a trade route to India, and in the process he discovered that the world was round. He did not put the cart before the horse.

Take any given experience and, rather than making a judgment, look for similar experiences that form a pattern. It's like a company doing consumer research on a product for a food manufacturer. They analyze the product. The customer tries the product, and they process the evaluations of the customer's opinion about that product. They then manufacture the product, and when they bring it to market, it doesn't do as well as they had hoped. I am not saying that process is totally invalid, but there is a better approach. Consider the possibility of having no product, and instead starting with a consumer need or interest. Then, as I said previously, analyze the application of the need, rather than the product. If you do that, you create a snack food rather than grocery products. You create a snack food that squeezes into your mouth and you call it a meal, because you realize in analyzing needs that the consumer is interested in meals to go. You realize that the convenience of snacking more frequently means that the snack becomes the meal, and then you are able to come up with a product that meets that specific application needs.

> ***Target Practice:*** Create a list of questions for your products and services. Start by taking one specific product and come up with its question.

13 Intuition Can Lead the Horse to Water, but...

The identification of a pattern though intuition can prompt you to study the implications of it, but mere study is not enough. While being a great student is important, smart people strive for more than that, they become scholars of their intuition. Follow their lead: don't become a generalist in your studies; become a specialist. Get to know the subject area revolving around, your bullseye, so specifically and so in depth that you read and study everything connected to it.

One of the most popular attractions in the state of Wisconsin is the House on the Rock. But it isn't the actual house that amazes most people who go there. It's the collection of all kinds of things that its builder and founder, Alex Jordan, collected over his lifetime and brought to that location as entertainment for people who came to see the House on the Rock. Jordan amassed the largest collection of miniature circus displays in the world. He became a scholar of the circus. He put together one of the largest displays of organs anywhere in the world. He became a scholar of organs. He acquired the largest, most elaborate merry-go-round in the world. He became a scholar of merry-go-rounds. Every time his intuition found something that interested him, he would read everything he could. He would study everything about that specific subject, whether it was doll houses or the Titanic. The key to being a scholar, a professor once told me, is to follow the thread. Go where it goes. For example, when you read something and it mentions a reference to someone or something you are interested in, follow that lead. It's like detective work. If you are going to be in the resort business, read everything, study everything, talk to every specialist, every guru, on how to run and develop a resort. Get to know everything you can. The advantage is that it helps you aim at the bullseye.

Truth: Those who know the customer best have the best chance of being the market leader.

Get smarter about what you are doing. Become a scholar who studies the needs and peculiarities of your customers to the point where you know things about them that no one else knows. Get to know what they want, what they like, why they came, why they come back, and what you could be doing differently.

Target Practice: Make a list of as many characteristics of your best customer as you can. See how many things you can list.

Market Smart? Take the BULLSEYE Quiz...

4. Intuition is:
   A. An outgrowth of experiences.
   B. Something people are born with.
   C. Are isolated experiences.
   D. None of the above.

5. One of the ways to be smart about your organization is to:
   A. Quite comparing yourself to others.
   B. Identify your strengths and weaknesses.
   C. Focus on the purpose for your product.
   D. All of the above.

Answers: winninger.com/bullseyequiz

IDENTIFYING FALLACIES

14 Fallacy: Entrenched Thinkers Are Smart

Recently I worked with an automobile brake manufacturer in Detroit. Actually, the company had invented the technology for the ceramic brake. The ceramic brake gives the performance automobile customer tremendous enhancement. It is cleaner and quieter. This brake manufacturer was supplying brakes to the original equipment manufacturers (OEMs). that is, the Big Three auto makers, who purchase everything based upon price, competitive bidding, and requests for proposals. The OEMs' buying process treats most things they purchase as commodity, and the manufacturer was losing profit margin. The members of the engineering department were called together, along with the sales department, to strategize as to how they could more effectively position themselves among the Big Three in the marketplace. But the engineers stalled in their thinking and spent most of their time trying to figure out how to defend the quality of their product and the fact that they had been first to market with the ceramic brake. They were entrenched in thinking about where they came from and fell into the trap of defending their deteriorating territory.

Entrenched thinkers aren't smart. They are too busy trying to keep things the way they were in a market, a place where things will never be the same again. The next time you conduct a smart think session, make absolutely sure that the room is not full of entrenched thinkers. Another name for them could be "turf managers," people who want to protect where they came from by defending the good decisions and smart thinking they have done in the past. When I facilitate thinking smart sessions, I make sure that no think group is made up predominantly of representatives from any given department. When the group is made up of a variety of departments, people with different responsibilities, it breaks up the territory managers, or entrenched thinkers, so that they can't support each other's thinking practices.

There is a great example of this in European history, when the Barbarians were attacking a bastille. The people in the bastille had been entrenched for well over four weeks and were running low on food. The Barbarians could not penetrate the bastille but persisted, thinking that eventually the people held hostage inside would give up or starve to death. When those in the bastille realized that they were running out of food and would either die of starvation or give up and be slaughtered by the Barbarians, they decided to put their thinking caps on and came up with another alternative. "Let's throw several bags of grain over the wall," suggested one smart thinker. "It will cut our rations in half and eliminate a couple days of our life, but the Barbarians might think we have plenty of food so that we can stay entrenched for a longer period of time. Maybe that will make them give up." He was right. That's just what they thought, and just what they did. Great thinking. Smart thinking. Risky thinking. But the people in the bastille were successful. Knowing that they were going to perish either way, they chose a different alternative. The alternative was creative. The challenge for many of us is that when we're entrenched, the fear and anxiety we bring to the decision-making process limits the alternatives we come up with for solutions.

Truth: Entrenched thinkers aren't typically smart.

Target Practice: List five statements that demonstrate entrenched thinking about your product or market. Prioritize them according to biggest challenge.

15 Fallacy: A Narrow Set of Alternatives Increases Creativity

Entrenched thinking limits smart thinking because its territorial protection strategy limits the possibility of alternatives, resulting in a low level of creativity. One of the most important steps in smart thinking is to develop a number of questions and then pare down the questions to those that focus on potential core answers. Another step is to come up with as many alternatives as possible. As the people confined in the bastille realized, when your two original alternatives are both hopeless, maybe you need a third alternative. Ask yourself what other alternatives you have that might afford more risk, but give you a better potential outcome.

There are not many elevator manufacturers left in the United States, and those that are still around know each other pretty well. Some great stories have come out of the elevator history books. One of those relates to a speed problem and the smart thinking that led to successful alternatives which hadn't been thought of before. A high-rise building developer was receiving a number of complaints from people in a new building about how long it took the elevators to get to any one floor. He called in a team of engineers and consultants specializing in elevator operation. They made suggestions like, "Speed up the elevators" and "Alternate the elevators by floor, odds and evens, or select several elevators to go to the higher floors and several elevators to go to the lower floors." Anyone who has traveled extensively to hotels in large cities has experienced these alternatives.

In terms of the added expense to the just-completed project, the developer decided that none of these suggestions were viable. Knowing that he was dealing with human nature, he decided it might not be an elevator problem as much as a people problem. He called in a psychologist, who analyzed the situation by comparing it with other buildings whose elevators were successful in moving people. The psychologist also came to the conclusion that the problem was a people problem, specifically, a waiting problem. If people have nothing to do while they're waiting, the normal human tendency is to exaggerate the amount of time it takes. While it might be only a minute, it seems like five minutes. The psychologist in this well-known story suggested putting mirrors across from the elevators on each of the floors. The developer accepted this as a low-cost way to at least attempt a solution and, *BULLSEYE!*, it was the right one. Almost immediately, the complaints subsided. Now, this doesn't mean that you can offer slow elevators and expect that simply by installing mirrors across from them you will be able to avoid complaints. Also, adding signs and posters that catch people's attention have proved to be an even lower-cost alternative to solving the problem.

Fairview Hospital in Edina, Minnesota, faced a similar problem with its admitting process. The solution? Rather than making people come up to a counter where they have to stand in line waiting to be admitted, the hospital has introduced hosts who greet the people at the door or in the lobby and take as much information as possible while they walk with them toward the admissions desk. People enjoy this enhancement. There is a bank on the east coast that does the same thing. They take employees out from behind the counter and put them among the customers on the floor, creating alternatives. An innovative approach like this achieves many things, but most important among them is that, because people appreciate the responsiveness and the care of businesses willing to cater to them, they will reward those businesses with their loyal patronage. It's similar to Jim Lind's service station where people are greeted on the lot by service station employees who wave and create conversation. Jim Lind has discovered things about his customers that he wouldn't have known if he hadn't created such interaction. And it has helped him tailor his services to their needs, assuring that they will come back again and again.

> ***Target Practice:*** Challenge your associates to suggest as many alternatives as possible to a single situation. Realize that the process is not to think, write, and then rethink that alternative. It is to think of an alternative, write it down, and then think of another alternative and write that one down.

Then go back and think through the alternatives, deciding which are better than the others and which have possibilities, but still need some additional thinking.

16 Fallacy: All Customers Are Customers

Believing that everyone who buys your products or uses your services is a customer is a fallacy that causes a lot of companies to miss not only the bullseye, but the entire target. Not all customers are customers; some are only transactions. If someone buys something from you once, never buys from you again, and never refers anyone else to you, why do you spend so much time trying to figure out what you could have done to make that customer happy or what other products they might have bought from you? There is a difference between a stakeholder customer and a transaction-only customer. Many companies ask the right questions of the wrong people; they waste a lot of energy and resources asking great questions of the transaction-only customer.

Hotels are typical. Whether it is Marriott or Hilton, there has been a trend over the years to pass out customer satisfaction cards. I like to refer to them as customer non-satisfaction cards. You are checking out, and they hand you a card and ask you to fill it out. Or they leave it in your room, or they put it on your food tray. "Let us know what you think of us," it says. I have always believed that there are people who are unhappy all the time, always responding negatively when asked to respond. Wouldn't it be frustrating if all the cards you got back were from people who were unhappy? I have come to the conclusion that happy customers don't fill out the cards. As I mentioned before, you're not smart if you are giving your customer opinion card to everyone who buys your product or service. If you were a hotel and you had a person staying fifty nights in your hotel properties versus a customer spending one night in your hotel, I would suggest that you profile those customers differently. The one who has the most frequency has the real relationship to you. This person is truly your customer, or your guest, as they say in the hotel business. The response from the person who stays one night in the hotel should be grouped with responses from others who only stayed one night. Responses from those spending fifty nights fit into the group of your most frequent guests. But by nature, the hotels, like most companies, pool the responses together.

Your customer stakeholder stays with you the most and refers other people to you. He'll tell you when he's unhappy, but he shouldn't be given a card to do it; he should be asked personally. Who has developed loyalty with you, willing to spend a little bit more for some of the extras? Who plans his relationship with you in advance, and doesn't just show up? So who are you most concerned about? Who should you seek to satisfy first? Market leaders are concerned about the stakeholder customer first. I have always said that the one you want to contact first is the one you can't afford to lose.

17 Fallacy: If They Like You, They Will Be Loyal

Truth: Customers aren't loyal because they feel good; they are loyal for a tangible reason.

Those who say that loyalty doesn't exist anymore are wrong, but loyalty today is not a warm, fuzzy feeling. Loyalty is not based on whether or not a customer likes you. It is based on something so tangible that it can be defined, measured, and clearly stated.

You need to cultivate relationships with your best customers. Market leaders don't leave loyalty to chance. It costs too much to lose one of your best customers. You need to make sure you know why they came to you, why they stay with you, and what you could be doing for them that you are not already doing. Those are the three critical things you need to find out from these customers. What brought them to you in the first place? Was it your location? A premium offering? Someone who directed them to you? A frustration they had with a competitor or someone else offering what they claimed was a similar product? An advertisement? Why have they been loyal to you? Put another way, once they came and experienced what you had to offer, why did they come back? Was it a person who worked for you who maintained the contact? Was it the quality of the product or service? Was it the way you sold them the product? And finally, ask the question that builds creativity for the future: What can else could you be doing for them? As I said at the outset, you need to be constantly researching your stakeholder customers, the people who are truly interested in a relationship with you and those potential customers who might be interested in a relationship with you.

> **Target Practice:** Make a list of the reasons your best customers come to you and stay with you, as well as the additional things you could be doing for them.

18 Fallacy: There Are Average Customers

Anybody who has been involved in market intelligence surveys or systems (MIS) has come to the realization that when they take all the statistics compiled on consumer preferences and average them together, a customer profile is identified that doesn't exist.

Truth: The average customer doesn't exist.

There *are* no average customers. Your average customer doesn't exist. If you use averages of your numbers, you have really created a customer that doesn't exist, or at least a rating that doesn't exist. The same thing happens when companies try to take averages of sales or sales per customer, put all the numbers together and you come up with a fictitious figure, or a fictitious customer. Most companies have three kinds of customers: frequent customers who come to you on a regular basis and tend to buy more from you or who refer other customers to you; customers who you wish would come to you more often but who shop around; and customers who seldom come to you, and then only when you are offering a good deal. Make separate composites of those three groups and keep the ratings or research within those subcategories, and you will get closer to the real wants and the real needs of a real customer. The other way to achieve this is to build a specific customer profile, to identify the type of customer you are seeking to satisfy. You can't just ask anyone what they think and contemplate their answer. The mistake is taking a universal survey of everybody you have done business with and asking them what they think. A car rental company should realize this when it really wants to know the uniqueness of its customers and what its best customers want. If you are a rental car company looking to be smarter about growing a profitable business, don't just survey any customer throughout a seven-day period of time, but rather a midweek traveler, arriving on a Tuesday and departing on a Thursday, who prebooks ten to fifteen rentals a year, and you will gather better information, getting closer to the bullseye.

> **Truth:** The tighter the profile of the targeted customer, the higher the quality of the resulting information will be.

If you don't want to operate based on information that results from averaging, watch the range of the numbers within the surveyed group that tend to be tighter, and this will get you closer to the real opinion of a real customer. I call this the "congestion factor." It's what developers do when they are looking for a great site for a new restaurant—they watch for traffic patterns. Whenever you look at numbers or do research, look at where the numbers or responses get congested.

> **Truth:** If you know what kind of customer you want, you will find more of them.

> **Target Practice:** Build a matrix of the characteristics of your best customer, the customer you wish all your customers were

like. Where did they originally come from? What do they buy? How often do they buy? What do they do with what they buy? What do they ask you for that you don't offer? How do they buy?

19 Fallacy: If You Like It, They Will Like It

Many people miss the bullseye because they assume that the customer who is buying their product or service is just like them. It's a fallacy if you are judging your product and service for your customer. A friend of mine, Tony Alessandra, wrote a book called *The Platinum Rule*. The book doesn't say "Do unto others as you would have them do unto you," it says "Do unto others as they would like you to do unto them." Unfortunately, many companies miss this bullseye because they assume that their attitude about the product or service is the customer's attitude about the product or service. There is still a valid reason for focus groups and advisory councils made up of the best customers. Many companies who realize they should be asking the customer what they think simply ask them questions, the answers to which support the company's erroneous position. Some companies even fall into the trap of asking people like themselves what they think of the product or service, or ask people who feel a responsibility to agree with the person asking the question. "Do you like our product?" "Sure, I like your product." Is this a true or false statement? And what does "like the product" mean? All information requests that build a foundation of thinking smart must bore deeper to get answers that are more revealing than "Gee, I just like it" or "It's a great day" or "We had a great time" or "We appreciate the quality of your product." As I said previously, all terms should be defined. Whether you use the term great, excellent, or satisfied, all of these are mere terms, but the definition of them is the answer to making smart decisions. In any case, you and your friends are probably not the right ones to ask about your product or service or the characteristics of a market and its needs. The closer you can get to the real customer's profile, the closer you will get to the information that will bring clarity to making smart decisions. Sometimes the best answers come from people whom we probably wouldn't seek to take to dinner. And the answers might hurt a little bit.

> ***Target Practice:*** Make a list of questions you would ask your best customers about your product or service.

20 Fallacy: Know Your Product Then Look for Your Market!

It is apparent that many companies who develop a product and then search for a customer for it are just ideas seeking a marketplace.

> **Truth:** Having a market that is seeking a product is more effective than having a product or idea that is seeking market validation.

This basic truth of marketing for the aspiring market leader: own a market segment that is seeking a great product, not a great product seeking a market. Thinking smart works the same way. It is smarter to have a great question that is seeking an answer than to have a great answer seeking a question. We have all met people who are convinced they have all the answers, yet have never been successful. They have a habit of asking you for a response to a question for which they have already formulated an answer. Let's take home delivery of groceries as an example. Even today, such companies as Simple Simon in Minneapolis, Minnesota, work diligently to create energy behind the concept of home delivery. It's an idea seeking an answer. Perhaps the question should be, "If people don't want to shop at a grocery store, what is the best, most convenient way to satisfy their need to shop for groceries?" As opposed to, "Hey, home delivery of groceries is a great idea. How can we get people attracted to the idea? How much energy and money do we have to put behind selling that idea?" In the course of any given year, hundreds of ideas are shared with me by people who just have a better way to do something or a new invention, a product or service that they just know everybody will want if somebody will give them the money to produce it or provide it or promote it. In any one of these situations, I apply my truth of market momentum, and that is, it is better to have a market interested in a product than a product interested in a market.

The online auction marketplace eBay has been phenomenally successful. Why? Because it knew a lot of people had a lot of junk, I mean, collectibles and uniquely valuable items. These people had a need for a way to sell their no-longer-needed items. eBay was a great answer to a great question: "How do I get rid of my stuff?" Martha Morris, the founder of Play It Again Sports, had the same question. She needed a way to get rid of her barely used sporting items, i.e. backpacks, hiking shoes, tent, and camping equipment. The answer was a garage sale that turned into one of the largest sporting goods retailers in the United States. Are you a person with a great question looking for an answer or an answer looking for a question? Do you have a market that needs a product or a product that needs a market? Market leaders all have a question in search of an answer. If you want to be one of them, make sure you have a market in search of a product.

> **Target Practice:** Ask one hundred of your best customers what they need that they can't find anywhere else. Make a list of things that customers ask for that aren't available.

21 Fallacy: Homogenous Groups Produce the Best Results

My wife says the best parties are made up of people from different backgrounds who didn't know each other before the party. It is the same in group think sessions. The industrial revolution changed the way we do things. The mental revolution changed the way we see things. The machine age thinking process was to cluster people and items by like characteristics, and we are still making that mistake. Thinking became siloed. The engine department was separate from the bumper department that was separate from the marketing department. We thought that we should separate the engine problems from brake problems and stability problems. The convergent systems approach doesn't think of parts;

it thinks of a whole, a system. We never would have put a person on the moon if we would have had to address the situation as components. If we don't think "system" today, the cell phone will continue to be the cell phone that we are always trying to find rather than a communications port. Today, the way to think smart is to look at the entire whole as a system. Do not silo the thinking process within your company. Many companies have not figured out that bringing the salespeople together in one meeting, the engineers in another, the production people in another, and the distribution people in yet another meeting will result in a machine age approach to problem-solving rather than a systems approach.

Some people refer to overview thinking as looking down from fifty thousand feet. You get the lay of the land. You see how things fit together. You see the effect of making a decision in one area and the effect it has on another area: the part versus the whole, the egg versus the chicken, or better, the chicken versus the hen house or the hen house versus the farm. Most companies have also found that customers are more interested in a overview approach. Not what it is but what it does! They are more interested in the application of the product than in the product itself. Show me how it works, show me what it does, they say. The machine age thinkers think that science and technology can solve every problem. So they apply science and technology to every situation. The overview people understand that there is a human component to everything, and if human nature fights science or fights technology, it often wins. The strongest thinking environments bring together people from all silo departments, all areas of the company, into a composite. When group think sessions are siloed, the result is constrained rationalism, limited thinking. You must get unconstrained by trying to understand what is going on in the other areas that are affected by your specific area of expertise.

> ***Target Practice:*** Make a list of the people from different backgrounds and different functions who should participate in your next group think session.

22 Fallacy: Products and Ideas Are Sold

After years of helping market leaders increase sales, I know it is a mistake to believe that products are sold. Products and services are bought for both the right and the wrong reasons. Those buying products and services are people, and people are human beings. Remember, there is a human factor in everything we do. We can create a pill to solve a physical problem, but we've got to get the human being to take the pill to solve the physical problem. The human factor affects everything, and we must adjust our constrained thinking by the human factor. Small armies with poor weapons have won battles against large armies with sophisticated weapons because of the human component and constrained thinking. George Washington finally won against the British in the Revolutionary War not because he had a better army or stronger regular army, but because he had a huge supportive component of a volunteer army that was capable of moving through the swamps and the lowlands and breaking the fighting system of the British.

> ***Target Practice:*** Think of all the human factors that affect the purchase and use of your product.

23 Fallacy: There Is One Right Answer

The challenge for all of us is that we were raised in a school environment where we learned how to find just one right answer, inadvertently losing the ability to look for more than one right answer. The challenge in thinking smart is that there could be more than one right answer, depending on specific situations. In thinking smart, once you have a right answer, look for another right answer. Once you have another right answer, look for yet another right answer. If you are answering the question of how to become a market leader, there could be many right answers. One would naturally be to create a new product, another might be to create a new way to sell that product, and yet another might be to add related products to your original product, such as accessories that become a part of it. Some right answers naturally would be more right than others. What qualifies one right answer as more right than another? It could be time, it could be uniqueness, it could be simplicity, it could be accessibility to the customer. I would suggest that if you want plural answers, you should ask plural questions. For example, rather than asking, "What is the right answer?" make it plural and ask, "What are the right answers?" Once you have come up with a number of different answers, prioritize them in terms of which seems to be the most right.

> ***Target Practice:*** The best way to get a right answer is to come up with a lot of right answers. Develop this process into a drill. Challenge your group to come up with five right answers, to one question!

Market Smart? Take the BULLSEYE Quiz...

6. Entrenched thinkers:
   A. Try to protect their territory.
   B. Make better decisions because they know so much.
   C. Become great resources for making decision.
   D. All of the above.

7. Which of the following is a true statement?
   A. If customers like you they are loyal
   B. Some customers are average.
   C. You should know your product well before you seek out customers.
   D. None of the above.

Answers: winninger.com/bullseyequiz

LISTENING SMART

24 Smart Organizations Pay Attention to the Changing Needs of Their Real Customers

People who think smart discover things because they heed the whispers of the market. They read between the lines. Do you pay careful attention to what your real customers are saying? What are your customers asking for that you don't offer? Are you isolating those requests for things that you don't offer? The biggest mistake most companies make when organizing focus groups is that those groups are not made up of the primary profile customers they are seeking to serve. These companies try to be everything for everybody, so they put everybody in their research project. Often, there is no discernment over who will be asked to fill out a questionnaire or who will be surveyed by phone.

It's like a political election survey that includes anybody and everybody. Who they would vote for and why is irrelevant if the people being surveyed aren't even going to vote in the end. So those who will not be going to the polls are influencing the attitudes of the people who are going to the polls.

The key to thinking smart is to gather relevant information, that is, information from a profile so well determined that the conclusions will be true. But researching opinion is only one small part of the equation. I have found that the truly smart companies are focusing more of their efforts on understanding the changing needs of their profiled customers and less time on evaluating the opinions of their current customers or what their competitors are doing. Why not institute a simple process where anytime a customer asks you for something you aren't offering, you write it down. Then drive the level of understanding a little deeper by asking your customers why they are asking about that specific thing, how they would use it, and where else they have found it? There are other things you could ask, too. Why didn't they think of you first? What would they be willing to pay for it, or what are the price sensitivities of their budgets? All of these things tend to help us think smart and to find the bullseye.

While one fast food place was looking for the beef, the other was trying to figure out who its best customer was and to identify that customer's highest changing need. The result was the Happy Meal. McDonald's identified its best customer as two adults in the front seats of a van, with children in the back seats, at a drive-through. The question that needed to be answered was this: "What do I give the kids to eat that they each will with be happy with and that I can order without having to think about it?" McDonald's took a burger, fries, a drink, and a simple toy, stuffed it in a bag, and called it a Happy Meal. Billions of Happy Meals later, the truth of smart thinking on the part of the folks at McDonald's is apparent.

25 Ask for Intelligence and You Will Be Smarter

The first step in thinking smart is to profile your premium customer, the person who is best served by your product or service. Then you make that customer the foundation of everything that you do. Seventeen percent of every market tends to be premium customers. They seek both product and service from the same location. Premium value is the name of the game with them. They will ask about the value before they will ask about the price. These premium customers are the movers and shakers of your business—the "17 percenters," as I call them. They aren't necessarily the wealthiest customers in your market, but rather the ones who calculate total value before they calculate total price. They are also the most loyal. As I have emphasized before, there are three questions that have helped businesses differentiate themselves and be smarter about what they do:

- Why did you come to us?
- Why do you keep coming back to us?
- What could we be doing for you that we are not doing for you now?

Whenever you have an opportunity, ask your customers these three questions. Then apply the frequency rule. When you find a frequency of request for things you could be doing that you are not doing, use that information to get your creative juices flowing and analyze how you would package those things into a service or product that can become a valued add-on to what you are already doing.

When Patterson Dental asked dentists what the company could be doing for them that it was not doing, the dentists wanted to talk about practice management. They wanted to talk about the future needs of their dental practice based on the changing needs of the dental patient. They didn't want to spend time worrying about the stocking of items and supply chain management. They wanted to talk about dental practice operations and what services they should be providing to their dental patients. They wanted to talk about what Patterson Dental knew or had discovered about the delivery of services that would affect the growth of their practice. When you ask for intelligence, you get smarter.

> ***Target Practice:*** Build a research project around the three questions above. Identify one hundred customers that fall into the profile discussed in this section. Ask them the three questions and tabulate the answers. Bring together a small steering committee group to develop a plan of action for implementation.

26 Listen Up—The Secret's in the Asking

You're missing the clues. Most companies would be smarter just by listening to customers and building a process for tracking what they hear. How many times on any given day is your company contacted for a product or service that you don't provide? It is not my intent to suggest that you follow each one of these requests by a potential customer with an idea that you think will help you be different or make you smarter in the marketplace, where everybody is copying everybody else. But I would state that the repetitive nature of the requests does merit recognition.

Imagine the difference it could make if on any given day, the people in your business picking up the phone, or in the field serving customers, or talking to customers in the store environment would quit responding to requests by saying, "No, we don't carry that" or "No, I'm sorry, we don't do that" or "We've never done that" and would instead say, "Gee, that's interesting. We don't currently offer that product. Why are you asking? What do you use it for? What size do you need?"

Listening to customer requests and tracking their repetitive frequency are two important steps toward becoming smarter about your business, but it doesn't stop there. There's much more to the process. First of all, you must identify the customer behind the request. Is it one of your real customers, the ones you are seeking to serve? Or is it a customer that you are not seeking to serve? Then, determine the customer's depth of need. How often do they purchase the item? What's their motivation? What's their budget for an item like this? Why did they think of you to ask? How soon do they need it? Finally, figure out what's missing.

Is there something more or different that you could be offering? These are all questions that lead to converging information, forming patterns that fan the flames of intuition and creativity. The answers will help you decide whether to reformat your approach to the customer, upgrade your business, change your business buying process to attract a different type of customer, or simply enhance what you are doing for your current customer. The whole process is truly nothing more than the ability to see the obvious in a repetitive pattern.

For example, on the basis of repetitive patterns it tracked among its customers, Best Buy reformatted its stores, to appeal more to the female consumer. Does your product or service appeal to the customer you are seeking to satisfy, or the one you are trying to get away from? Are you using an order-taking process for sales in the field to serve a customer who really wants a consulting approach? Or are you in the field trying to consult with customers who just want to place an order? The ability to track requests will add to your intuition.

27 Smart Questions Lead to Smart Answers

Throughout this entire study, I continually emphasize your ability to ask questions that lead to smart decisions. Everybody is full of ideas. I have always said that I don't need one more idea to make me successful or make me rich. I need an idea that's attached to a truth. Questions we all need be asking to be successful in business include: "What business am I in?" "How do I define the business I'm in?" "What is the mission of the business or idea?" "What should the mission be?" "Who is our prime customer?" "Who should our prime customer be?" You will notice that in each of these questions, we are not asking ourselves about the needs we serve today, but rather about the potential for the future. "What is the products perceived price to value relationship to our customer?" "What need does our product serve?" "What changing need does our product serve?" "What growth market has a need for our product?" Any of these questions can be applied universally.

Those who got caught in the technology trap failed to ask the right questions. Perhaps they failed to ask the questions because they refused to face the reality of having a product that cannot be driven through technology, when today all products need to be touched with some technology to enhance their value and usability and responsiveness to the customer. But remember, it's not just the asking of the questions but the clarity we bring to the answers to these questions that is important. As I have said before, if you want answers, you need to ask the right people.

> **Truth:** The clarity and quality of the answer is diminished by the diversity of the profile of those being questioned.

A number of years ago, I was asked to lead some focus groups for one of the largest retail grocery chains in the United States. It was obvious to me at the outset that the way the focus groups were profiled by this particular organization violated the principle, the truth, that I have just shared. In any given room, they would bring together young married couples without children, young married couples with children, older married couples who were empty nesters, and seniors. They would ask the same question of each of these different types in hopes of getting a composite answer. Well, depending upon what composite means, and I would like to think it is relevance and quality, all of the people around that table trying to answer the same question should have been of a similar profile rather than four or five different profiles.

Most of the focus groups in this experience ended up in debate over what was important to whom. The company doing the survey should have taken into consideration that the grocery needs of these different groups vary greatly and cannot be composited into a single focus.

We all make the same mistake. I have watched meeting planners pass out cards to an audience made up of middle managers and salespeople and upper management, and then ask them to complete a questionnaire that failed to qualify each of them as to their position. Any composite from such a questionnaire would be irrelevant. If you are going to do research at all, be smart enough to build a profile that gets you a quality composite. That doesn't mean you can't have three profiles, but ensure that when you are creating the composite, you separate the data from each of those groups.

> ***Target Practice:*** Identify three profiles of customers for your product. List three questions that you would ask each of the groups. Identify how the answers might vary based on the uniqueness of the groups.

28 Wrong Question, Wrong Answer

It's easier to judge the past than the future. When organizations are headed down the wrong path, they tend to continue down the wrong path. This has been referred to as "staying the course." This happens because they are asking the wrong questions, and the wrong questions result in the wrong answers. For example, the company that decides to cut the cost of a sales transaction ends up cutting the sales force and over the long term ends up with declining gross revenue. It is interesting to note that this has been a very common occurrence in the past few years, because companies selected a cost-cutting strategy rather than a revenue-generating strategy. Not to confuse you, but in a matrix you can ask the wrong question and get the right answer. You might not know it, though, because your question was wrong. This happens because the people involved lack experience or are too protective of their position to recognize the right answer when they hear it. The right question for the past few years has been, "How do we grow market sales and revenue in a tough market?" not "How do we cut costs?" I will cover this in more detail the next Bullseye Book, but in short, the simplest way to increase revenue in the short term is to cross-sell your products to increase the revenue from each transaction. Your goal is to keep the customer from buying *one thing* from you and another thing from your competitor. It's also smart to realize that most salespeople are simply taking orders rather than growing the business with each order. If the whole concentration of your business is on a salesperson taking orders, then technology will quickly replace that person and you!

I am amazed that so many companies view the challenge of a flat or negative market as a time to cut costs rather than to grow business. My father, who was in the real estate business, always reminded me, "Do the things that other people are not doing and you will tend to grow your business even in the toughest markets." If everyone were cutting costs, pulling back on training and advertising, and closing offices, the strategic position would be to enhance your product, grow the business, entrench your salespeople in effective training, and vertically integrate your product. To vertically integrate your product is to increase the average per customer sale by connecting accessories to your product so that the customer, thus growing your margin. How about snow skis and poles with stylish winter outerwear against a rustic mountaintop ski lodge background? How about the fishing pole with the tackle box, fishing waders and jacket? The "less is more" maxim does not apply here!

Let's say, hypothetically, that you are in the mattress business. When a customer enters your store, all they see are mattresses and box springs shoved as close together as they can be to get as much product on the showroom floor as possible, mattresses all lined up in a row with price tags and a sign that says, "If you are interested, ask us."

Well, you say, we're not in the retail business, we're a distributor. Does that mean that your catalogue is also crammed with stuff that doesn't sell often? What the emerging premium customer today is looking for is a lifestyle. They are seeking to buy products whose usability or desirability is obvious. With that in mind, it would be wise to display the product in an environment where it is connected to its application or to other products that are part of its application. Lifestyle customers want to see the product in the environment where they will use it.

A very successful Milwaukee-based, custom-crafted sleep products organization in the midst of a flat mattress market took a big step and created a "collections" group, so that when people purchased the mattress and the box springs, they would naturally purchase the coordinating pillows and other items of bedding. The company increased their gross revenue by 6 percent, which in this particular case was well over three million net dollars. I have often said that if asking questions is the way to generate more store traffic, perhaps the questions could be, "How do we increase the closing ratio of our salespeople in the stores?" and "How can we build a new buying model so that our customers are captured by the uniqueness of how we bring the product to them, rather cutting costs or spending a lot more money to increase traffic in lousy stores?"

> ***Target Practice:*** What can you do to increase your average customer purchase? How could you ask the customer to spend a little bit more, and what would they spend a little bit more for?

29 Start with the Questions

If we were going to put together a strategy for being smart, it would be comprised of several steps. But one of the most important things would be starting with the questions. Making a list of questions. Identifying the value of the questions. Prioritizing the questions in terms of the most important ones to be answered. Evaluating the questions from the customers' vantage point or from an outcome position. Jump ahead three to four years down the road and ask yourself, "Looking back, was this question the most important one I could have asked? If not, what question should I have been asking?" The eight-track tape manufacturing company should not have been asking, "How can we more effectively produce a high-quality eight-track tape?" They should have been asking, "What technologies will affect the future viability of eight-track tape recorders, and how quickly will they be replaced?" They would have changed their focus immediately and might not have gone out of business.

As an exercise, put two or three independent thinkers together and just list questions related to your market and your product. Questions like "What is the marketability of our product over three to five years?" "What things are happening in the marketplace that could threaten the viability of our product?" "How do we grow margin, not just grow sales?" "What are the core skills our people need to have to effectively sell our product?" "How can we differentiate the buying process for our product in the marketplace?" "What can be attached to our product to differentiate it, that is, what accessories can become part of our product?" As the result of asking better questions, the airlines have changed the way they do business. They have better adapted to the lifestyle of travelers booking their own trips. The airlines have changed the buying model. When you call for a reservation now, they will offer you rental car services, hotel services, and a number of other miscellaneous services that enhance the value of the trip and ease your planning. This change by the airlines has challenged travel agencies to shift from just booking travel to offering comprehensive trip planning. Their focus is to enhance the total experience of your trip by putting together everything it takes for you to say, "Wow!"

> **Target Practice:** How can you change the way your do business to bring it more in line with the needs of you customer? Think about what you can add to what you are already doing for the customer so that they will say, "Wow!"

30 Single Response Questions Kill Creativity

Some thirty years ago, I graduated from Marquette University with an undergraduate degree, with emphasis in broadcasting journalism. One of my instructors, John Grams, told us that if we wanted to be great journalists, we would have to get the critical facts that others overlooked. To help us do that, Professor Grams taught us to ask open, probe rather than closed, probe questions. I discovered later in my career that it truly was a concept of getting smart, not just a concept of communication. The goal is to discover what other people don't know. The same thing applies to being smart, asking the right questions that lead to creativity. Asking closed-probe questions that can only be answered with a "yes" or "no" stifles creativity, because it limits the depth of what you learn. Asking open-probe questions that begin with who, what, where, when, why, or how excite and enhance creativity, because they draw out a depth of information.

For example, rather than asking customers, "Do you think that our store is big enough?" ask yourself, "If we expanded the floor space in our store, what premium products would we merchandise there that would be attractive to the customer and generate more per-square-foot revenue?" There is a total difference between these two questions. Another example: "Should we add the capability to our Web site to transact business?" Well, the answer can only be "yes" or "no," versus, "If we did that, what kinds of customers would be drawn to purchase from our Web site?" "How do we create a long-term relationship with a Web site customer?" "What value does that bring to our other sales efforts?" All open-probe questions. Smarter questions.

For years I have told the story about coming home from a trip and saying to Lynne, my wife, "Do you want to go to the movies?" That question doesn't enhance smart thinking from knowledge collection creativity. Her only response could be "yes" or "no" or "I don't know," and typically, being an analytical person, her response was the latter. The real question is, "Honey, if we were going to go out tonight, what would you like to do?" An open-probe question develops a better long-term relationship. "Should we go to the beach?" versus "What beach should we go to?" or "If we went to the beach, what would you like to do?" Truly, asking better questions that lead to deep responses is a technique that enhances our ability to think smart in all situations.

> **Target Practice:** Make a list of open-probe questions that lead to a depth of understanding of the needs, wants, and motivations of your primary customer.

Market Smart? Take the BULLSEYE Quiz...

8. Market leaders:
   A. Satisfy the needs of their customers.
   B. Study the changing needs of their primary customers.
   C. Track the needs of the people who could be their customers.
   D. Know what they should do to improve their old products.

Answers: winninger.com/bullseyequiz

USING
THINKING TOOLS

31   Get with the Tools

There are many tools you can use to enhance your ability for making smart decisions, which in the end will help you hit the bullseye. One of the simplest is something I refer to simply as "scan." Take a piece of paper and draw two vertical lines on it, making three columns. In the first column, write all the positive responses to a specific question. In the second column, list all the negative responses to the same question. In the third column, list all the interesting responses, that is, those which are neither positive nor negative. For example, if you asked the question, "What would happen if we raised the price of our primary product?" a positive response would be, "We would generate a higher margin in each transaction." Another positive response would be, "We would get our customer's attention focused on why we are asking for more money" (i.e., because the product is worth it). A third positive response would be, "We would feel better about we are doing." A negative response might be, "The number of customers buying our product might go down." Another negative response is "With the reduction in numbers of transactions, our gross earnings would go down." And yet another would be, "But if we are attempting to sell the same product for a higher price, our customers will say we are crazy." In the third column, under interesting responses, we might say, "It would be interesting to see if we attract a better customer." Or, "It would be interesting if people appreciated us more because of it." Or perhaps, "It would be interesting to see whether the attitudes of our customers would change about the value of our product." I call this "scan" because you are really looking at three ways to answer a single question, and when you have these answers, you can look across the lines to see what the variances are.

People have suggested to me that the "scan" approach is nothing more than a mechanical way to stimulate creativity in a group that isn't normally creative. Yet all of us need stimulation, and all of us need direction. Stimulation can come from a thought pattern or a process that we put ourselves into. There is reason why people go on retreats and sabbaticals to empty their minds. They do it so that they can get focused, so they can let some of the creativity rush in. The "scan" approach is a simple process of challenging people to identify ways of finding different answers to the same question. Having done this for many years, I find that the groups who isolate a single factor or a specific question about their business tend to be more effective. Those who stay general in nature, attempting to look at the good, the bad, and the interesting for their overall business, tend not to be as successful. Those who look at a color, a number, a product, a service, or a type of customer tend to be more effective because they are really getting to the heart of the business and can get much more specific in terms of their responses. Most smart people move from general to specific. The closer we can get to clarity and specifics, the higher the quality of the outcome we get from the process.

We must be reminded, however, that it is not good enough to just come up with pages of ideas. It does no good to simply make lists of possibilities and never do anything about them. We must move to what the *one thing* is. Identify the *one thing*, out of all the possibilities, that seems to be the most relevant to a given situation or seems to be the most dramatic to a given situation. Changing the color of something from blue to purple, for example. Purple might be a bigger risk than yellow or red, but you are willing to take it because it differentiates you in the marketplace, or based upon the parameters of the question it seems to be the most plausible action in terms of where you intend to go. The "scan" approach really should be applied in two steps. One step is to focus on the primary outcome of the scan itself, the good, the bad, and the interesting. The other is to judge the reactions you get to the statements from the scan. It is very similar to drawing a picture and then having everybody identify what the picture means to them or what the picture says.

> ***Target Practice:*** Do a three-column "scan" about something that you have been considering, like adding a product or a service. Remember, column one is the positive responses, column two is the negative responses, and column three is the "It would be interesting..." responses. As a final step, ask for reactions to the column statements.

32 Be Team Smart, Not Just Self Smart

When people get together to be creative and look at possibilities, it is important to create a formal framework. Devote one minute to defining the target or task, two minutes to exploring and expanding, and three minutes to contracting and concluding. In this case, let's say the target is to create a better way to answer the telephone. Results usually come very quickly. Most groups can, in less than one minute, define a target or a task. Make sure you use the full minute, however, and don't jump off to other targets and tasks. Then, use two minutes to expand and explore. How many ways are there to answer the telephone? Well, we could have a telephone answering machine; or a person could pick up the phone by the third ring. How about giving customers specific access numbers that allow them to get through to specific customer services representatives? For example, Northwest's Platinum customers have a special code they can use when they call the airline's frequent traveler hotline. That code gets them through to a person who understands that they are very frequent travelers. The code also triggers the technology to access the traveler's account.

Finally spend a couple of minutes contracting and concluding. That is the process of deciding specifically what you are going to do as a result of this thinking process. When thinking smart, you need to apply a specific process and a specific time in which to do it.

Truth: Different people see things differently.

When you assemble your creative group, limit it to just four or five people who can work together. Having a small team with a single focus will produce a better outcome. If the people in the group are all from the same department or represent the same specialty, the thinking won't be as creative. Diverse groups, groups where people come from different departments, will see the problem from several different angles and tend to get better results. There have been many studies done on relationships between people, and most of them show that when people are of different natures, but enjoy some of the same things, the relationship seems to be stronger and deeper, because each one points out certain things to the other one that he or she did not notice, enriching the experience.

Target Practice: Practice the thinking exercise. In a group environment, devote one minute to defining a target or task, two minutes to exploring and expanding, and three minutes to contracting and concluding.

33 Now You See It, Now You See It Again

It has become obvious in all my years of working with smart people and observing smart people that pattern recognition is a significant way to appear to be thinking smart and, in fact, to actually end up thinking smarter.

> **Truth:** Recurring things or patterns lead to positive projections.

Recurring things that get noticed sometimes tell a great story about an opportunity. A national overnight shipping company starting recognizing a pattern of customers calling to track where their package was in the shipping process. Hotel chains noted the frequency of calls to the front desk by business travelers looking for an iron and ironing board. Jim Lind noticed that almost every time he gave full service to a person at a self-service pump, the car needed some kind of lubricant. A well-known consultant discovered that people didn't just want to hear how to be smarter; they wanted to find out how smart they were by taking a smart quiz. Patterson Dental discovered that whenever they had an opportunity for one of their people to talk to a dentist, the dentist wanted to talk about trends in the business. Each of these cases represented an opportunity to serve the customer better.

Target Practice: What recurring patterns have you observed in the way you do business or the way the customer reacts to you?

Market Smart? Take the BULLSEYE Quiz...

9. Scan is a:
    A. Tool for thinking smart.
    B. Way to compare the positive and negative responses to the same question.
    C. Way to speculate what would happen if something what true.
    D. All of the above.

10. If your organization is going to be a Market Leader:
    A. You need some smart people on your team.
    B. The whole team needs to work on thinking smart.
    C. You need to look for isolated situations where your organization has been smart in the past.
    D. All of the above.

Answers: winninger.com/bullseyequiz

ACHIEVING FOCUS

34 Change the Rules

In the early seventies, one of the top collegiate basketball teams in the United States was Marquette University, which, as I mentioned previously, is my undergraduate alma mater. At that time, Al McGuire was the coach. Al had many great sayings—too many to repeat here. But one I attribute to him that I will never forget is a statement he made to his team before every game: "Guys, we are going to go out on the floor and play our game. It's our game! When the other team learns our game so well that they can play our game, we'll change our game." Numerous interesting facts about collegiate basketball can be traced to legend Al McGuire. The box rule for coaches is one of them. Al would walk the whole floor and coach his team in front of the competition's bench. He also used a designer, so goes the story, to have the basketball uniform changed. The professional teams today wear a uniform that was a takeoff of that uniform.

The key message in all of this is: change the rules. Gutenberg changed the rules, and the world, by creating the printing press. The printing press, according to the history books, was really nothing more than a wine press. The wine press became a word press and put books in the hands of the average person.

I made the stark realization a number of years ago that most companies limit their growth because they follow the rules. Every year, sales departments of companies project annual increases in sales based upon what their sales were last year. They follow a predictable time line based upon a matrix of the economy and a few other simple characteristics, as well as a predictable increase over the last ten to fifteen years. Companies mistakenly state their goal for the coming year based on some percentage over the previous year. Let's say, for example, that each year you raised your goal 5 percent, saying, "Well, we did it last year, so we can do it again this year. The economy is about the same." Think of how you stifle your true potential, though. Perhaps your potential is 10 percent, based upon the skills and core competencies of your talented people. You've done a better recruiting job and your staff is more excited about getting customers excited about your product and service.

Truth: Predictability limits thinking smart.

But you continue to increase your annual projections based on some vanilla, no-risk format. You are limiting your future based upon predictability. I suspect if I give you a series of numbers, 1, 4, 9, 16, 25, 36, that you could give me the next three numbers in sequence. That's right, 49, 64, 81. And all you are doing to predict those numbers is establishing the add-on difference between each of the numbers by an odd number.

> **Target Practice:** What rules have you been following that you would like to change or break? How would the change affect your industry? If you have difficulty thinking of ways to affect your industry, think of other industries that have been affected by someone who changed the rules.

35 Premium Payoff Priority

Think of the biggest-bang-for-the-buck concept. What can be the greatest growth we can have for the smallest investment? I call this the "premium payoff priority." If it is the right priority and there is a premium payoff, it must be connected to an overriding objective, or "big bang." The overriding objective would be to dramatically increase the number of repeat customers. The premium payoff priority is the *one thing* or action that will cause this to happen. When qualifying the priority, there are three things to consider: What will give you the greatest return for a minimum investment? What will get a strong buy-in from all the players? What will achieve a specific benchmark goal? In a repeat customer situation, what is the *one thing* you can do to stimulate the greatest number of repeat transactions in a short period of time? Come up with as many ideas as you can, and then apply a market intelligence system. If you can only choose one of the ideas, the market intelligence system identifies which of them would best satisfy your three criteria: the biggest bang for the buck, the easiest to implement among the team players, and the one that is most attractive to the customers. Hotels have found that when it comes to the business traveler, quick check-in drives more repeat sales than almost anything else. In the grocery store, it is fast checkout and ease of shopping.

> ***Target Practice:*** Make a list of the premium payoff priorities that you have experienced in your business—the little things that have made a big difference.

36   Get Smart about Customers

Market leaders today know their customers better than anybody else. They know who should be their customers. They have found out that if they are going to be successful, they have to get as close to the customer as possible. What are the customer's needs and wants? How do they frame those needs and wants? How do they identify different types of customers within their segment? What are the changing customer needs? Market leaders are constantly listening to, identifying, and responding to what they see, hear, and observe in customer contacts. They are reaching outside their customer base to analyze the needs, wants, and motivations of potential customers. They are constantly studying the use of their products and services to know how they relate to normal human thought processes and behaviors. *I need mobility. I need a car. But I want a sports car. No, I want a red convertible sports car. My motive is ego satisfaction. I need food. I want fast food. I want Hispanic fast food. I want chipotle flavor. I want to be around upwardly mobile young adults. My motive is social interaction and fun.* Each customer revolves around three degrees of attachment, needs, wants and motives.

> **Truth:** If you don't know your customer's motive, you are not close enough to your customer.

Market leaders understand that the bullseye is motive, and they discover it by moving in with their customer.

> **Target Practice:** Take your core product or service, the one main reason your customers come to you. Identify their needs, then identify their wants, then identify their motive.

CONCLUSION

There is no conclusion to think smart. It is a continual process of indentifying and clarifying opportunities of delivering value to the key customer segments that afford you or your business a leadership position. The overriding objective is to create a differentiator that gains a unique market leadership position satisfying a purpose for existence. The most important differentiator in any business is thinking smart. If you can gain focus and zero in on the *one thing*, you will by nature make better decisions, create sustainable success, and build efficiencies of scale.

PREVIEW OF BOOK TWO: *BULLSEYE!* CREATE VALUE

Now that you have started thinking smarter, thinking differently, and making better decisions, it's time to aim at the next *BULLSEYE!* book, which is *Create Value*.

This second volume in the three-part series is not so much a think book as it is a concept book. There are fourteen bullseye imperatives, concepts that market leaders use to consistently hit the mark. Naturally, each concept is based on a *Truth*. With each bullseye imperative, there will be an example of market leaders who use the concept effectively. To get a pre-publication Copy of Book 2 *Creative Value...* winninger.com/bullseye

BRING THOM WINNINGER IN FOR YOUR NEXT CONFERENCE AND MEETING

3 Exciting Presentations

Create Value!
How to Create Priceable Value!
Create tangible and priceable value
Which Market Leaders always get full price
8 Imperatives in the new economy
Capture *trends* with *actions*

Think Smart
How to Think Like a Market Leader!
Make Better decisions the first time
Target Trends
Get closer to shifting markets
Become more innovative

Build Culture
How to Build a Culture of Difference!
Create a *Corporate Genetic Code*
How Market Leaders sustain success?
What to do besides "try harder"?
Bring the team in line with the culture

Get a FREE Audio Program of
Winninger Speaking Live at winninger.com

or CALL 1-800-441-5510
To Book a Speaking Date